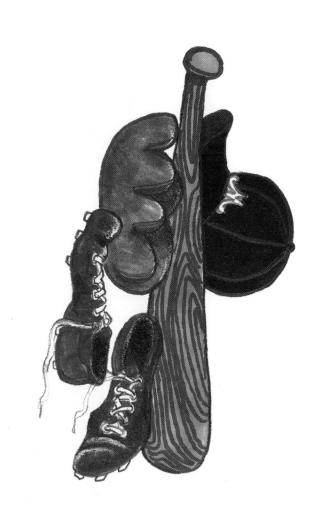

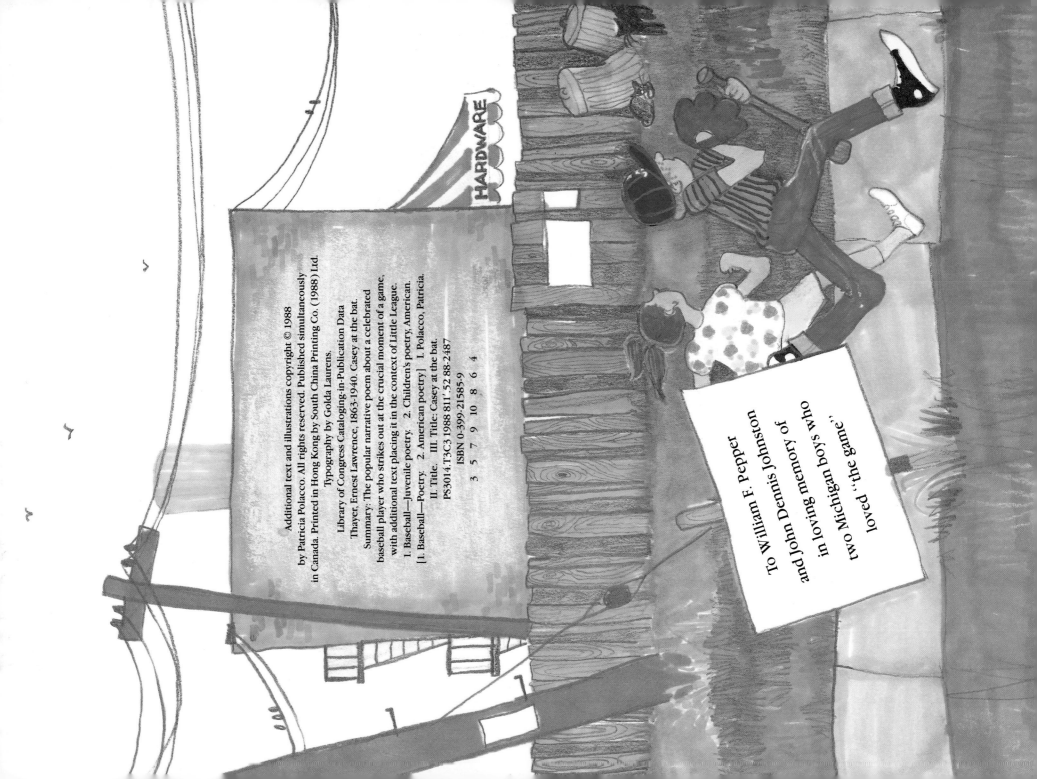

Additional text and illustrations copyright © 1988 by Patricia Polacco. All rights reserved. Published simultaneously in Canada. Printed in Hong Kong by South China Printing Co. (1988) Ltd.

Typography by Golda Laurens.

Library of Congress Cataloging-in-Publication Data
Thayer, Ernest Lawrence, 1863-1940. Casey at the bat.
Summary: The popular narrative poem about a celebrated baseball player who strikes out at the crucial moment of a game, with additional text placing it in the context of Little League.
[1. Baseball—Poetry. 2. American poetry] I. Polacco, Patricia.
II. Title. III. Title: Casey at the bat.
PS3014.T3C3 1988 811'.52 88-2487
ISBN 0-399-21585-9

3 5 7 9 10 8 6 4

To William F. Pepper
and John Dennis Johnston
in loving memory of
two Michigan boys who
loved "the game"

G. P. Putnam's Sons
PRESENTS

Casey At The Bat

A BALLAD OF THE REPUBLIC,
SUNG IN THE YEAR 1888

Ernest Lawrence Thayer

With additional text and illustrations by

Patricia Polacco

G. P. PUTNAM'S SONS · NEW YORK

"Casey, aren't you supposed to be at the big game today?" Connie asked her brother.

"Oh, I'll get there in time—I'm the star hitter, ain't I? They can't win without *me!*" he answered arrogantly.

"Casey, remember what Dad always says: 'Be on time. Always play your best. Don't count your hits before they're pitched—and do it fair and square.'"

"Hey, I'm the best!" he growled.

"Best or not—it's three o'clock."

"THREE O'CLOCK! THE GAME! C'mon, Connie! We're LATE!"

"Yer late, kid!" the umpire barked.

It was Harry Donovan, the meanest, leanest, keenest ump in the Little League. Of all people to see Casey arrive late! Donovan had a murderous look in his eye as Casey and Connie ran into the stadium.

Casey's fellow teammates were none too cheerful either. . . . .

The outlook wasn't brilliant for the Mudville nine that day:

The score stood four to two, with but one inning more to play,

And then when Cooney died at first, and Barrows did the same,

A pall-like silence fell upon the patrons of the game.

A straggling few got up to go in deep despair. The rest

Clung to that hope which springs eternal in the human breast;

They thought, "If only Casey could but get a whack at that—

We'd put up even money now, with Casey at the bat."

But Flynn preceded Casey, as did also Jimmy Blake,
And the former was a hoodoo, while the latter was a cake;
So upon that stricken multitude grim melancholy sat,
For there seemed but little chance of Casey getting to the bat.

But Flynn let drive a single, to the wonderment of all,
And Blake, the much despised, tore the cover off the ball;
And when the dust had lifted, and men saw what had occurred,
There was Jimmy safe at second and Flynn a-hugging third.

Then from five thousand throats and more there rose a lusty yell;
It rumbled through the valley, it rattled in the dell;
It pounded on the mountain and recoiled upon the flat,
For Casey, mighty Casey, was advancing to the bat.

There was ease in Casey's manner as he stepped into his place;
There was pride in Casey's bearing and a smile lit Casey's face.
And when, responding to the cheers, he lightly doffed his hat,
No stranger in the crowd could doubt 'twas Casey at the bat.

Ten thousand eyes were on him as he rubbed his hands with dirt;
Five thousand tongues applauded when he wiped them on his shirt.
Then while the writhing pitcher ground the ball into his hip,
Defiance flashed in Casey's eye, a sneer curled Casey's lip.

And now the leather-covered sphere came hurtling through the air,
And Casey stood a-watching it in haughty grandeur there.
Close by the sturdy batsman the ball unheeded sped—
"That ain't my style," said Casey. "Strike one!" the umpire said.

From the benches, black with people, there went up a muffled roar,
Like the beating of the storm-waves on a stern and distant shore;
"Kill him! Kill the umpire!" shouted some one on the stand;
And it's likely they'd have killed him had not Casey raised his hand.

With a smile of Christian charity great Casey's visage shone;
He stilled the rising tumult; he bade the game go on;

He signaled to the pitcher, and once more the dun sphere flew;
But Casey still ignored it, and the umpire said, "Strike two!"

"Fraud!" cried the maddened thousands, and echo answered "Fraud!"
But one scornful look from Casey and the audience was awed.

They saw his face grow stern and cold, they saw his muscles strain,
And they knew that Casey wouldn't let that ball go by again.

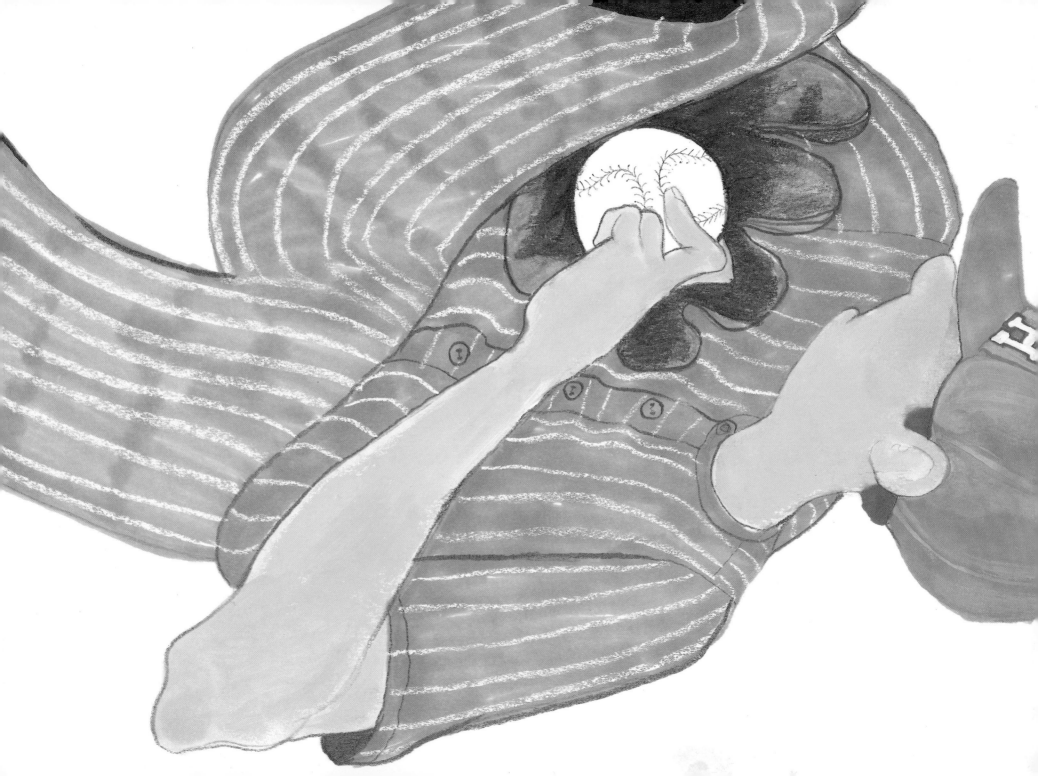

The sneer has fled from Casey's lip, his teeth are clenched in hate;
He pounds with cruel violence his bat upon the plate.
And now the pitcher holds the ball, and now he lets it go,

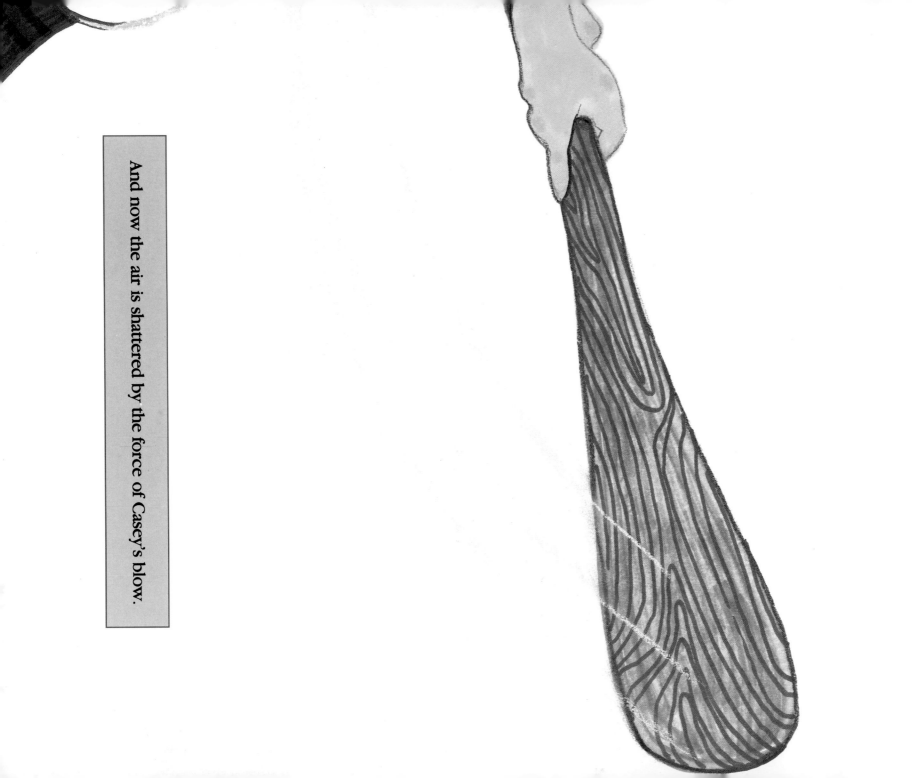

And now the air is shattered by the force of Casey's blow.

Oh, somewhere in this favored land the sun is shining bright;
The band is playing somewhere, and somewhere hearts are light.
And somewhere men are laughing, and little children shout;
But there is no joy in Mudville—mighty Casey has struck out.

"Sorry, Casey," the umpire said. "But I calls 'em the way I sees 'em."

"Aw, it's ok," Casey answered softly. "I was struck out fair and square. Guess I was counting my hits before they were pitched, huh, Dad?"

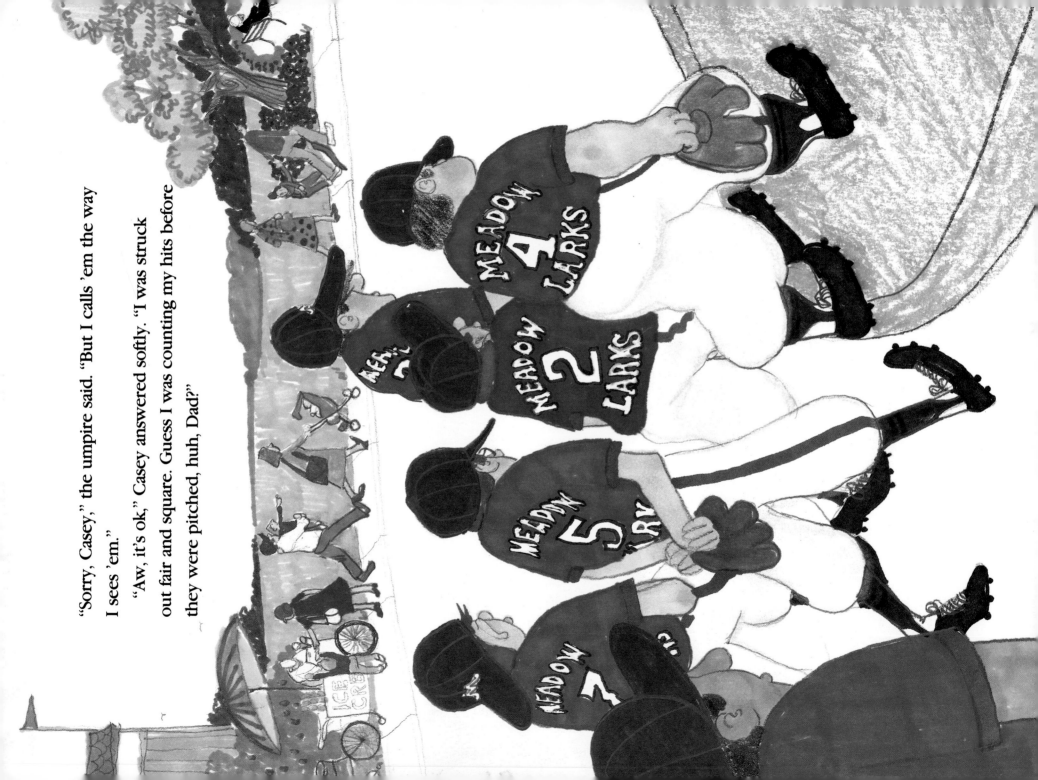

"C'mon, kids. Let's go home and see what's for dinner."